IMAGES
of America

VIRGINIA-HIGHLAND

"Virginia-Highland" emerged in 1972. Faced with the prospect of a highway that threatened to destroy the community, a small group fought back, created the Virginia-Highland Civic Association (VHCA), defined the neighborhood's boundaries, and inspired a spirit of hope. Mary Drolet designed the original VHCA logo to symbolize a new day dawning in the community of single-family homes. (Courtesy of Mary Drolet.)

ON THE COVER: The commercial district at the corner of Highland and Virginia Avenues was bustling in 1949. Moe's & Joe's Tavern was established in 1947 and is a popular gathering place six decades later. (Courtesy of Special Collections and Archives, Georgia State University Library, Elliot and Sara Goldberg.)

IMAGES
of America

VIRGINIA-HIGHLAND

Karri Hobson-Pape and Lola Carlisle

ARCADIA
PUBLISHING

Published by Arcadia Publishing
Charleston, South Carolina

Library of Congress Control Number: 2010943236

For all general information, please contact Arcadia Publishing:
Telephone 843-853-2070
Fax 843-853-0044
E-mail sales@arcadiapublishing.com
For customer service and orders:
Toll-Free 1-888-313-2665

Visit us on the Internet at www.arcadiapublishing.com

This book is dedicated to Carli, Parker, Sierra, and the future generations we hope will treasure this neighborhood for years to come.

CONTENTS

Acknowledgments

Our heartfelt thank-you to Judy Potter, our outstanding research partner and editor. Your passion about history and our community has provided constant inspiration. This book could not have been completed without you.

Pierce and Tommy, thank you for letting us escape to do what we love as you held down the fort.

Carli, Parker, and Sierra, you are great researchers. May you and your friends always appreciate your special neighborhood.

Jack White, thank you for your countless hours of editing, advice, and contributions to the neighborhood we have today.

This book was put together with the help of hundreds of people who have shared their stories, time, and passion. Thank you for building such a wonderful community!

Greg Abel for your generosity of spirit and space, Camille Wolf for your meticulous support and never-ending curiosity, Linda Merrill for first writing the history for the Historic Preservation exploration, Mary Davis for your insights and leadership, Caitlyn Zygmont, Robert Catron, Tom Catron, Barbara, Curtis, and Joe Cheshire, Lucy Crenshaw Kelly, Joseph Drolet, Doris and Ray Hildebrand, Ramona Liddell, Albert Martin Jr., Adele Northrop, Reshma Shah, Patrick Almand, Mike Andriola, Chris Bagby, Sharon Bagby, George and Judy Beasley, Jerry Bright, Warren Bruno, Sandra Spoon, Margaret Calhoun, Helen Cassandras, Jennifer Chambers, Mary Chance, Stephanie and Tom Coffin, Judy Cohen, Tracy Crowley, Brad Cunard, Winnie and Sonnie Currie, Robin Davis, Mary Denmark Hutcherson, Sharon Dennehy, Lynn DeWitt, Ellen Dracos-Lemming, Mary Drolet, Jackie Fleeman Gramatas, Peter Frawley, Bennett Frisch, Virginia Gaddis, Cynthia Gentry, Elliot and Sara Goldberg, Jerry Greenbaum, Nancy Hamilton, Justin Haynie, Few Hembree, Robin and Wendell Hobson, Shirley Hollberg, Patricia Jayne, Cliff Kuhn, Susan Kraham, Howard Krinsky, Maria Isabel and Bill LeBlanc, Helen Lee, Trudy Leonard, Oreon Mann, Annie Marbury, Sheryl and Stuart Meddin, Maria Melissovas, Tom Murphy, G.G. Najour, Jackie Naylor, Gail Novak, Josephine Nunez-Gross, Karen Page, Pamela Papner, Martha Perimutter, Rick Porter, Jerry Reimer, Scott Sanders, Larry Santiago, Herb Schmidt, Jeanne Shaw, Chip Simone, Frieda Socal, Emily Swindall, Julia Valentine Weathers Wynne, Harold Vrono, Abbie Bordeaux, Geoffrey "Quatrefoil" Borwick, Conne Ward-Cameron, Mary Alice Ware, John Wolfinger, Kathy Yancey, Mike Zarrilli, Rabbi Zelony, Mark Arnold, Rosa Arriaga, John Becker, Jon Carlsten, Tracy and Win Carroll, J.D. Christy, Liz Coyle, Richard and Rosina Cunningham, Ann Tinkley Devlin, Marie Farrell, Rupert Fike III, Rob Glancy, Kim Griffin, Linda Guthrie, Martha and Van Hall, Scottie Johnson, Kathryn King-Metters, Jane and Andrew Lipscomb, Anne Mahaffey, Jill Marber, Judy McCabe Smith, Marylyn Morton, Barbara and Don Murphy, Martha Pearlmutter, Cindy Phelan, Sue Powers, Polly Price, Ron Rodriguez, Barbara Rosenblit, Denise Solomon, Scott Stern, Bonny Valente, Dowman Wilson, Emilie Wingfield, Herb Wollner, Jim Zwald, Roy Black, Libby Cates, Janice Giddens, Lillian Ann Grovenstein, Margaret Herrington, Elizabeth Marsala, Lloyd Mendelson, and many more.

INTRODUCTION

Atlanta's Virginia-Highland enjoys a rich history, a diverse urban fabric, and a distinct sense of place.

For nearly a century after the Creek Indians roamed this territory, it was farmland. Richard Copeland Todd settled with his family in 1823, near what is now Greenwood Avenue and Ponce de Leon Place, overlooking what eventually became the city of Atlanta. Rich land and family ties attracted Hezekiah and Sarah Cheshire, who settled farther north and planted fields of wheat, cotton, and vegetables. Slowly, schools and churches were built, as life in the Old South took shape.

The trauma of the Civil War devastated the community; battles were fought throughout the immediate area. The frontier families who returned after the war found little but charred chimneys and were forced to rebuild their homes and lives.

In the 1890s, trolley lines were extended northeast of Atlanta along the "Nine-Mile Circle," offering city residents access to the breezes of the higher elevations. The legendary medicinal waters of Ponce de Leon Springs attracted people to the region. Grand residences like the Adair home at the corner of Highland and Virginia Avenues hosted lavish summer parties for the well-to-do.

The agrarian environment faded in the early 1900s as the area's first subdivisions were built. The new developments offered affordable homes, mostly single-family bungalows, to a growing professional and middle class. A strong immigrant population, primarily from the Middle East, Greece, and Eastern Europe, settled in the region and established many local businesses. A new wave of industry arrived with the Ford Motor Company factory and the Sears retail distribution center along Ponce de Leon Avenue, prompting more single-family homes and multifamily units.

The community suffered a period of decline in the mid-20th century due to the lure of the suburbs, the impacts of integration, and a highway that was planned to cut through the neighborhood. What might have been a quiet transition to another generation was shattered by the Georgia Highway Department's announcement that a six-lane highway (I-485) would be constructed through the neighborhood. The road would have crossed parks, created a diamond interchange at the western end of Virginia Avenue, and obliterated hundreds of houses. Some demoralized families fled, but others fought back and were joined by a wave of new arrivals.

A small group of residents began working with other neighboring civic associations and formed the Virginia-Highland Civic Association to combat—and ultimately defeat—the highway plans. This presented the opportunity to consolidate the various subdivisions as Virginia-Highland and define the geographic boundaries of the community we know today. Strong community activists joined forces to halt highway construction and ensure the survival of the neighborhood. During the years of uncertainty, scores of middle class families left Virginia-Highland for distant suburbs. A new culture of activists, some involved in the antiwar and counter-culture movements, arrived in the neighborhood.

In the 1970s, young professionals and families began to move back into the city, renovating run-down houses and embracing intown living. New restaurants and boutique shops replaced the utilitarian businesses that had occupied the retail fronts in earlier decades.

Many of the same features that contributed to its initial development—access to the major business centers, excellent schools, bustling local shops, and an unpretentious culture—continue to attract new residents. A unique culture of spirited dialog and debate, part of the heritage of the highway fight, characterizes the community as it seeks a balance between a hip, vibrant commercial district and an enjoyable residential neighborhood.

One

THE GEORGIA FRONTIER

After the Creek Indians ceded the land, Richard Copeland Todd and his wife, Martha, journeyed from South Carolina and settled in the Virginia-Highland area. In 1823, they established their homestead on land covered in hickory, beech, and oak near present-day Ponce de Leon Place and Greenwood Avenue. They farmed in the area for the rest of their lives, raised five children, and were buried at the Todd family cemetery. (Courtesy of Mike Zarrilli.)

Prior to the arrival of the original pioneer families, Native Americans roamed the region. The Chattahoochee River marked the dividing line between the Cherokee Nation north and west of the river and the Creek Nation south and east of the river. The area surrounding Virginia-Highland was considered a buffer zone. In 1821, the Creek Indians ceded these lands. (Courtesy of Library of Congress: LSZ62-110850 Remington.)

A lottery was held to distribute land to "free white males over 18" who were Georgia residents of three years or more. Special rules were set for soldiers, widows, and orphans. The winners, referred to as "fortunates," claimed grants by paying $19. This image depicts the 1821 Land Lottery in Milledgeville, the state capital, as hopeful citizens pulled their tickets. (Courtesy of Cindy and George Parrish Jr.)

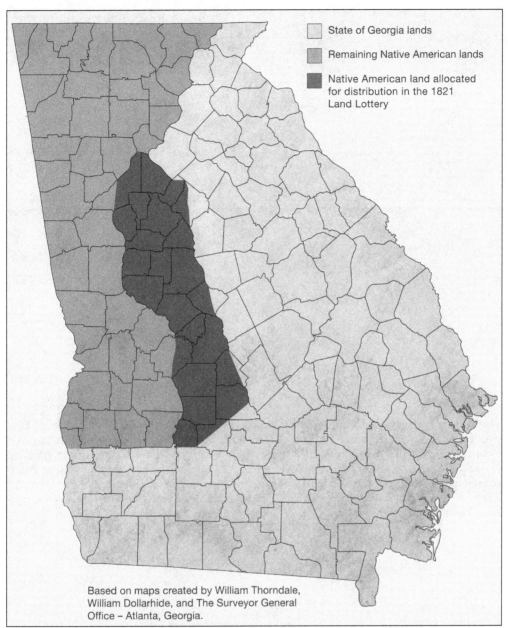

State of Georgia lands

Remaining Native American lands

Native American land allocated
for distribution in the 1821
Land Lottery

Based on maps created by William Thorndale,
William Dollarhide, and The Surveyor General
Office – Atlanta, Georgia.

The Treaty of Indian Springs on January 8, 1821, opened the portion of Georgia between the Ocmulgee and Flint Rivers for settlement. On May 15, 1821, the Georgia General Assembly divided the land into five large counties, including Henry (where Virginia-Highland is located), Dooley, Houston, Monroe, and Fayette. The lottery offered lots of 202.5 acres and took place in November and December of 1821. A year later, DeKalb County was formed out of Henry County. In 1853, Fulton County was formed to reduce the time required for railroad executives to get the necessary permits from the DeKalb County seat of Decatur. (Based on prior renderings by William Thorndale, William Dollarhide, the Surveyor General Office, Atlanta.)

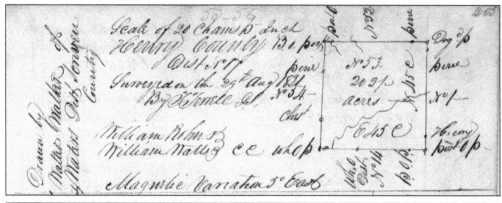

The current boundaries of Virginia-Highland comprise a portion of six different lottery land lots. These two plats show Land Lot 53 (District 17), drawn by Walter Walker from Screven County, Georgia, and Land Lot 17 (District 14), drawn by William Zachry from Columbia County, Georgia. William Zachry quickly sold his 202.5 acres, which extended from Adair Avenue to North Avenue, to Richard Copeland Todd in 1823, for a reported $100. All of the lots for this area remained intact with 202.5-acre parcels until the 1850s. (Courtesy of Georgia Archives, Office of Secretary of State.)

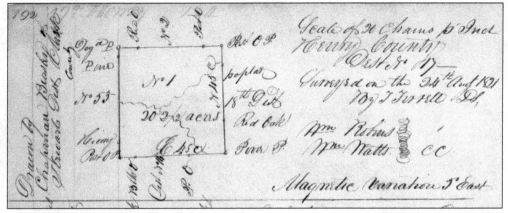

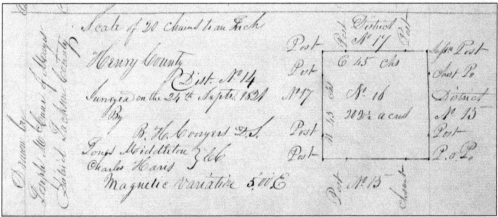

These original land plats show Land Lot 1 (District 17), which included the intersection of Virginia Avenue and North Highland Avenue, drawn by Chapman Beasley from Clark County, and Land Lot 16 (District 14) drawn by Joseph McCune from Jackson County. The other two lots to the east (not shown here) were drawn by John Wicker (Land Lot 1, District 18) and John Braddy (Land Lot 241, District 15). John Braddy was only 21 years old, barely exceeding the age minimum of 18. Many of the original pioneers bought land, sometimes sight unseen, from lottery winners. Records indicate that the original Land Lottery winners sold their land without settling in the area. Many made a handsome profit on their investment. (Courtesy of Georgia Archives, Office of Secretary of State.)

The first settlers in the 1820s and 1830s lived in tents and wagons until their homes were erected. Richard Copeland Todd and his wife, Martha, built their homestead on the high ground near present-day Greenwood Avenue and Ponce de Leon Place (which was initially called Main Street).

From their front porch, the Todds viewed the rolling hills. In later years, they watched the activity of the Ponce de Leon Resort and the ballpark that was built in the valley below. Four generations of the Todd family enjoyed this home until it burned in 1910. (Courtesy of Ramona Liddell.)

Richard Todd's sister Sarah married Hardy Ivy, who is often considered Atlanta's first settler. In 1833, the Ivys erected this log cabin near Piedmont Road and Ellis Street to live near Sarah's family, who had been in the region for a decade. In 1848, Hardy Ivy was thrown from a horse and died. Some historians believe that he was buried in the Todd family cemetery. (Courtesy of Kenan Research Center at the Atlanta History Center, Kurtz.)

The Todd family cemetery was between present-day Ponce de Leon Terrace and Drewry Street, west of Barnett Street. One of the area's earliest cemeteries, it had graves of both black and white settlers. Two homes have since been built on the plot. Martha Todd's gravestone, photographed above in 1980, has been removed. Residents reported that a developer periodically removed gravestones at night. (Courtesy of Ramona Liddell, Gail Novak.)

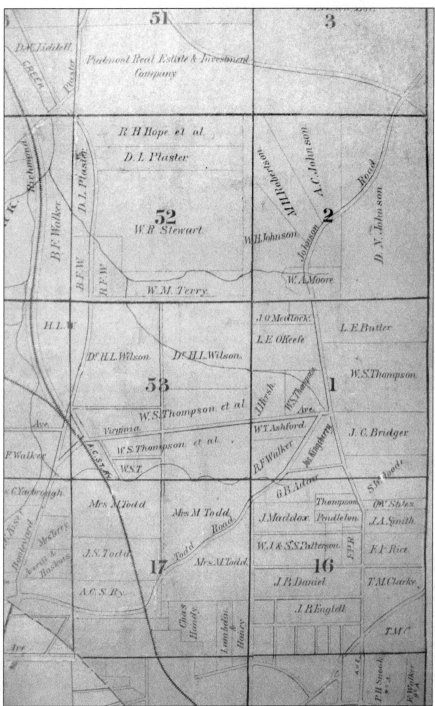

Todd Road is one of the oldest known streets in Atlanta. Clearly indicated on Civil War maps, it directly linked the homesteads of Hardy Ivy and Richard Copeland Todd. This 1893 map shows Todd Road continuing from Ponce de Leon Avenue prior to the extension of Ponce to Decatur. A small portion of Todd Road exists today. (Courtesy of Kenan Research Center at the Atlanta History Center.)

Harris Goodwin came searching for gold in the Georgia hills; he carried a satchel to collect gold for earrings for his sisters. He was joined in the 1830s by his father, Solomon Goodwin, from South Carolina. Solomon's daughter Sarah (left) married Hezekiah Cheshire in 1836 in South Carolina, and they journeyed to Georgia on horseback with a baby in arms. (Courtesy of Albert Martin Jr., *The Spirit of Rock Spring.*)

Sarah and Hezekiah Cheshire likely lived with her father, Solomon, when they first arrived in Georgia. Solomon Goodwin built his home on a 600-acre farm. It became known for its hospitality to travelers heading to Marthasville, later renamed Atlanta. Still standing at 3931 Peachtree Road in Brookhaven, it is the oldest existing house in DeKalb County. (Courtesy of Albert Martin Jr.)

Capt. Hezekiah Cheshire, born in Maryland, was a veteran of the War of 1812. He and his second wife, Sarah, 28 years his junior, built a home at approximately present-day 1186 North Highland Avenue on eight acres they purchased for $18. They had nine children and planted fields of wheat, cotton, and vegetables. Hezekiah was known for his hospitality and took great pleasure in entertaining both friends and strangers. He died in 1870 and was buried in the Plaster family cemetery. That year, Rock Spring Presbyterian Church was founded on the corner of Piedmont and Rock Springs Roads. Sarah and two of their daughters were founding members and are buried in the church cemetery. A marker has been placed there for Hezekiah. (Right, courtesy of Albert Martin Jr.; below, courtesy of Ellen Dracos Lemming; *The Spirit of Rock Spring*.)

This is a photograph of the Cheshire home on Highland Avenue (approximately present-day 1186 North Highland Avenue), with Hezekiah and Sarah's family in front. Though Hezekiah was too old to fight in the Civil War, four sons did. When the Union troops approached Atlanta, the Cheshire family left by train, with one cow in the freight car. Sherman's soldiers used their home as a hospital. When the family returned, nothing was left but a charred chimney and the graves of both Union and Confederate soldiers. In 1866, they built another home. The structure on the left housed a drinking well. (Courtesy of Barbara Cheshire, Rock Spring Presbyterian Church, *The Spirit of Rock Spring.*)

For years residents had made the then-lengthy four-mile journey to worship at the Decatur Presbyterian Church. After the Civil War, they formed the Rock Spring Presbyterian Church on Plaster's Bridge Road (now Piedmont Road) on land donated by James Washington Smith. The original white frame building (above) was completed in 1871. (Courtesy of Rock Spring Presbyterian Church, *The Spirit of Rock Spring*, The Johnson family, Emily Swindall.)

Daniel Johnson settled in 1824, building his homestead at the corner of present-day Johnson and Lenox Roads. Daniel, a clock salesman and founding member of Rock Spring Presbyterian Church, married Elizabeth Chandler, daughter of a prominent landowner. Highland Avenue may have been built along the ridge top as a route from Atlanta to their homestead. (Courtesy of Rock Spring Presbyterian Church, Barbara Cheshire, *The Spirit of Rock Spring*, The Johnson family, Emily Swindall.)

As the community grew, a place was needed to educate the children. The first school in the area, a one-room log cabin, was built in 1835 where the Rock Spring Presbyterian Church on Piedmont Road is currently located. After the war, the second Rock Spring School (above, around 1869) was built on East Rock Springs Road at the intersection of Morningside Drive. Homemade tables were used for desks, and slabs were used for seats. Children of all ages from the area attended, and there was one teacher for the entire school. Some Confederate veterans attended. According to a local family, the Plasters, the noon recess was a highlight and included horse-and-buggy races. (Courtesy of Kenan Research Center at the Atlanta History Center, Barbara Cheshire, *The Spirit of Rock Spring*.)

The Civil War significantly changed the life of these pioneers. Atlanta's outer defenses extended along Highland Avenue, and engagements were fought along Highland Avenue and Briarcliff Road, close to the Cheshire home. According to one account, breastworks were erected in front of the Todd house during a battle that took place over the valley between Ponce de Leon Place and Monroe Drive. (Courtesy of author.)

In 1868, ailing and sickly railroad workers discovered two springs, one freestone and one mineral, near the site where the Sears building was later built. The springs were originally used as drinking water; when the workers got healthy, they credited their recovery to the medicinal qualities of the water. (Courtesy of Kenan Research Center at the Atlanta History Center.)

The springs became a pilgrimage site that was developed into Atlanta's first health resort. Beginning at sunrise, city folks gathered to collect water. Henry Lumpkin Wilson, a prominent doctor and surgeon of the 7th Georgia Regiment during the Civil War, became the first city physician and was elected to the city council. In the lean years after the war, he accepted payment for services in eggs, butter, and chickens. In 1870, suffering from indigestion himself, Wilson visited the springs and named the source "Ponce de Leon Springs" after the Spanish conquistador known for seeking the Fountain of Youth. His home (below) was among the grand estates that lined Peachtree Street. (Courtesy of Kenan Research Center at the Atlanta History Center.)

The establishment of the Gentleman's Driving Club in 1887 (in what is now Piedmont Park) drew attention to the area northeast of the city. In 1895, the site was used for the Cotton States and International Exposition, the last and largest of three great trade shows the city held to showcase the South's recovery from the Civil War and promote trade. The exposition ran from September 18 to December 31, 1895. Frederick Law Olmstead consulted on the layout of its buildings and grounds. Shown are the Central Terrace (above) and the Agriculture Building (below). (Courtesy of Kenan Research Center at the Atlanta History Center.)

Two

FARMS AND
COUNTRY ESTATES

Born in 1847, Judge John C. Todd
was the youngest son of Martha and
Richard Copeland Todd. Too young
to serve with the Confederates, he was
raised at the Todd homestead, working
on the farm and ultimately taking a
leading role as Atlanta developed.
He is shown here in 1902 with his
grandson Heyward "Todd" Liddell
Sr. on the porch of the homestead.
(Courtesy of Ramona Liddell.)

Judge John C. Todd and his wife, Sarah Jane Mayson, raised two children, Heyward Todd and Emma May Todd. The surrounding community was still relatively small, and many of the original pioneer families were connected by marriage. In this photograph, Sarah Jane Mayson Todd (left) is shown with her sister Carrie Elizabeth Mayson Cheshire, who married Napoleon Cheshire, the son of Hezekiah and Sarah Cheshire. (Courtesy of Ramona Liddell.)

Judge John C. and Sara Jane Mayson Todd's two children, John Heyward (known as "Hadie") and Emma May, were born and raised on the Todd property. Hadie is remembered for his extreme good looks and his active social life. His family reminisces that he was often surrounded by beautiful women, yet he never married. Death records indicate that he died at age 42 in a private sanitarium. At right, Hadie is standing on the porch of the family home, between his father and a friend. He is in the back seat of the car below. (Courtesy of Ramona Liddell.)

John C. Todd and his son-in-law, Andrew "Drew" Pickney Liddell, both known by the (possibly honorific) title of Judge, held positions of prominence in Atlanta's white society. Judge John C. Todd is pictured at left with great grandson Billy Morgan, son of Ellen and Bill Morgan, in 1920. In his later years, John C. witnessed the development of the surrounding area. The Todds sold portions of their estate to various developers, which proved to be a great source of wealth. (Courtesy of Ramona Liddell.)

Drew Liddell (above left) married Emma May Todd (above right, in her later years). His parents, James and Piety Liddell, settled after the war at 464 Montgomery Ferry Road in a beautiful home that still stands today near the corner of Monroe Drive. Drew was very involved in the Masons, Shriners, and other prominent society organizations and was recognized as a judge in the community. They had three children: Sarah, Ellen, and Heyward Todd Liddell Sr., shown below riding his bike at the original Todd homestead when he was five years old. (Courtesy of Ramona Liddell.)

After the first Todd homestead burned in October of 1910, they built a large, two-story brick residence with a wrap-around porch at what is currently 816 Greenwood Avenue. The family referred to it as "The Big House." Members of the Todd family occupied it well into the 1950s, when it was sold and replaced by multifamily housing. Initially, Bonaventure Road continued to Drewry Street. In the late 1940s, Emma May Liddell (shown above with her daughter Ellen Liddell Morgan) asserted that the family owned the land and closed the street extension. (Courtesy of the *Atlanta Journal-Constitution*, © August 1949, the *Atlanta Journal-Constitution*. All rights reserved.)

The Todd family servants lived on a nearby dirt road known as Rooster Foot Alley. It descended from the Todd cemetery toward a small lake near present-day Ponce de Leon Terrace and Ponce de Leon Place. This community of small homes survived for many years, even after additional development in the 1920s. (Courtesy of Ramona Liddell.)

Lucy Crenshaw (above) was young in the early 1930s, growing up on Virginia Circle. She visited a family on Rooster Foot Alley with her father, who was providing legal assistance for an adoption. She remembers the homes as small and well-maintained. Prior to that occasion, she was not permitted near Rooster Foot Alley. Traditionally, white girls were not allowed to visit unaccompanied. (Courtesy of Lucy Crenshaw Kelley.)

In 1924, Heyward Todd Liddell Sr. married Bertie Sue Cheshire (left). The young couple spent a great deal of time in the Todds' "Big House" and was active in Atlanta's white high society. Bertie Sue led a life that made an impact on many fronts, including the women's suffrage movement in Atlanta. (Courtesy of Ramona Liddell.)

Bertie Sue Cheshire was the daughter of Clara Annie Fritz and Homer Mayson Cheshire. Her mother, Clara, grew up on land that is now Piedmont Park, not far from the Todd farm. Clara's father, John Fritz, sold a portion of his farm for the Atlanta Exposition. Clara's name may have inspired the name "Lake Clara Meer," the lake at the center of Piedmont Park. (Courtesy of Ramona Liddell.)

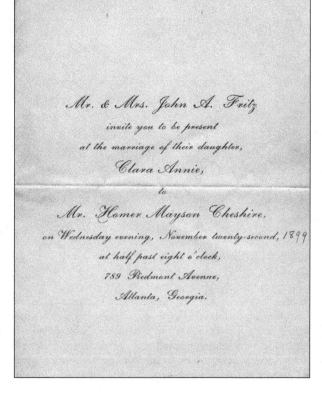

Mr. & Mrs. John A. Fritz
invite you to be present
at the marriage of their daughter,
Clara Annie,
to
Mr. Homer Mayson Cheshire,
on Wednesday evening, November twenty-second, 1899
at half past eight o'clock,
789 Piedmont Avenue,
Atlanta, Georgia.

As late as the 1940s, the Cheshire home was occupied by Hezekiah's maiden daughters Mattie and Sallie (right). For decades, the women lived simply, drinking from the old well in the front yard. In later years, they reluctantly accepted city water and electricity. Sallie presumably sold portions of the land, since the corner of Highland and Amsterdam Avenues was developed in the 1930s. (Courtesy of Albert Martin Jr.)

Hezekiah and Sarah Cheshire's sons Napoleon and Jerome built farms to the north along both sides of the North Fork of Peachtree Creek. The road connecting their farms became known as Cheshire Bridge Road. Napoleon Cheshire's home (below in the 1890s) was located near the current southeast corner of the intersection of I-85 and Cheshire Bridge Road. (Courtesy of Ramona Liddell, *The Spirit of Rock Spring*, Rock Spring Presbyterian Church.)

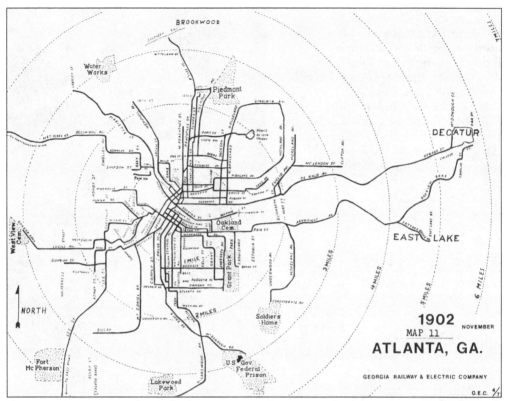

As streetcar routes moved outside the city center, the agrarian landscape dramatically changed. In 1889, the Fulton County Street Railroad Co. began service to the undeveloped land to the northeast of the city. Its route, the "Nine-Mile Circle," required the broad sweeping intersections that exist today at North Highland and Virginia Avenues and Virginia Avenue and Boulevard (now Monroe Drive). The Nine-Mile Circle was a popular excursion for Atlanta residents who enjoyed escapes to the wooded countryside on trolley "picnic cars" that sometimes featured brass bands. The city's two streetcar businesses consolidated as the Georgia Railway & Electric Company in 1902, when the map above was produced. (Courtesy of Georgia Power Corporate Archives.)

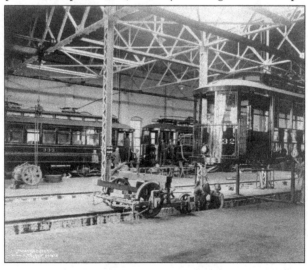

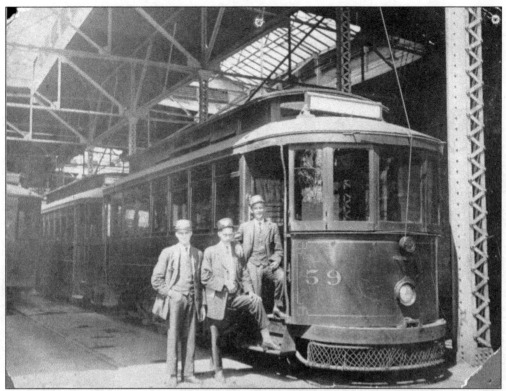

The Virginia Avenue Car Barns, built in 1888 near the intersection with Boulevard (now Monroe Drive), were long structures used for repairing and maintaining trolleys. New buildings constructed in 1906 included a foundry to forge metal parts such as wheels. This site became the primary shop for the street railway system and provided employment for many local residents. The shop produced the last streetcar in 1924, as the automobile gained in popularity. The car barns were used by MARTA as bus maintenance facilities until the 1980s, when they were torn down and replaced by apartments at what is now 609 Virginia Avenue. The creosoting facility is shown below in an undated photograph. (Above, courtesy of Vanishing Georgia, Georgia Archives, Office of Secretary of State; below, courtesy of Georgia Power Corporate Archives.)

One of the first grand homes in the area was built during the mid-1890s at 1000 Highland Avenue (now 964 Rupley Drive) by Green Buron "G.B." Adair and his wife, Adelaide. Set on 40 acres along the Nine-Mile Trolley line, it was initially a country estate used to escape the noise and congestion of the city. Expansive gardens extended all the way to Highland Avenue near its current intersection with Virginia Avenue. The elegant two-story, brick Spanish Mission–style house has a bilaterally symmetrical front facade with scalloped parapets. The home cost more than $40,000 and had an open first floor large enough for grand balls. Its once-grand front gardens are now homes and commercial buildings along Highland Avenue. (Courtesy of Ellen Dracos Lemming.)

Born in 1840 in Alabama as one of nine children, G.B. Adair (right) enlisted in Montgomery as a private in the Confederate infantry and fought for all four years of the Civil War. He was one of 16 men of the original company of 116 who survived to surrender on April 9, 1865, with Robert E. Lee at the McLean House (below) at Appomattox Courthouse, Virginia. After settling in Atlanta in 1866, Adair entered the wholesale fertilizer business with his brother Augustus "A.D." Adair and built Adair and Brothers Provisions. They were among Atlanta's most successful merchants and were key players in rebuilding the city after the war. (Right, courtesy of Doris Hildebrand; below, courtesy of Library of Congress: ppmsca12910, Timothy O'Sullivan.)

In 1875, G.B. Adair married Adelaide "Addie" Marsh, whose family was very wealthy. G.B. and Adelaide had three sons, G.B. Jr., Edwin Marsh, and Spencer. G.B. retired from active business in 1891, but remained active in Atlanta charities and business affairs. His civic activity extended to running for a City Council seat in 1897, an election he won by one vote. The *New York Times* article below, published in 1897, carried the news. Adair was remembered in his obituary as "one of Atlanta's most beloved citizens." He was known in the business world as "a man of sterling character, energetic, and progressive." Both he and his wife were buried in the Oakland Cemetery Marsh mausoleum. (Left, courtesy of Doris Hildebrand; below, courtesy of the New York Times Company.)

ELECTION IN ATLANTA.

A Single Vote in the Fifth Ward Decides the Government of the City.

ATLANTA, Ga., Oct. 9.—The municipal election held in this city yesterday was so close that a single vote decides it. The struggle for the control of the local Legislature was a neck-and-neck race throughout the city, and last night the returns gave three wards to each of the administration and anti-administration factions. The Seventh Ward was undecided.

In the Fifth Ward the struggle was between Green B. Adair and H. A. Boynton, and the friends of both put in a very hard day's work. The count of the ballots gave Adair 2,255 votes and Boynton 2,254.

To-day Boynton demanded a new count, which was made, but the result showed no change, and Adair was declared the victor by the margin of one ballot.

A score or more of people are laying a claim to the honor of casting the deciding vote. A prominent railroad official from Atlanta was visiting in Chattanooga, and came into town on a special train to vote for Adair. It is probable that his right to be known as the man who settled the contest will not be disputed.

As a young man, G.B. Adair Jr. (above, center) met Susie Conley (right), a Catholic girl from Atlanta known for her wonderful voice. As staunch Baptists, G.B. Adair Sr. and Adelaide forbade G.B. Jr. to marry a Catholic and threatened to disinherit him. Madly in love with Susie, he happily forewent the family fortune and wed her when he was 19. Without any family money, G.B. Jr. became a salesman at a local clothing store, the Keeley Company, and at radio station WSB, where he sold time. He later converted to Catholicism. Susie Conley sang at Sacred Heart Church for more than 25 years and was a professional opera singer. Despite the disinheritance, G.B. Jr. cared for his mother in her later years after the death of his father. (Courtesy of Doris Hildebrand.)

G.B. Jr. and Susie Adair lived in a bungalow on Boulevard, now 1218 Monroe Drive, near the intersection of Amsterdam Avenue, within miles of his childhood home. They had seven children, all of whom loved to entertain and had extraordinary musical talent. G.B. Jr. performed vaudeville on the weekends and began to travel throughout the country with his act. The family created a music group promoted as "The Seven Adairs" and was heard on radio throughout Georgia and beyond. Fans sent telegrams to radio stations asking for more airtime for The Seven Adairs. These family photographs were taken in front of their home; note the grassy median in the background on Boulevard (Monroe Drive). (Courtesy of Doris Hildebrand.)

Three

SUBURBAN DEVELOPMENT

The commercial buildings at the northwest corner of Highland and Virginia Avenues (above) were erected in the early 1920s. For many decades, Virginia Avenue was just one of several cross streets and was not commonly mentioned when referencing the area. Activity and traffic was oriented southward toward downtown, and residents referred to living "off Highland." This c. 1925 photograph looks north on Highland Avenue. (Courtesy of Larry Santiago and Bonny Valente.)

The growth of the city's streetcar system provided easier access to Ponce de Leon Springs, which featured an artificial lake for boating and swimming, an amusement park, picnic area, skating rink, and other attractions. Note the restrictions on "disorderly characters" and "colored persons" on the sign in the bottom photograph. (Above, courtesy of Witt Bros. Postcard; below, courtesy of Virtual Vault at the Georgia State Archives, Office of Secretary of State.)

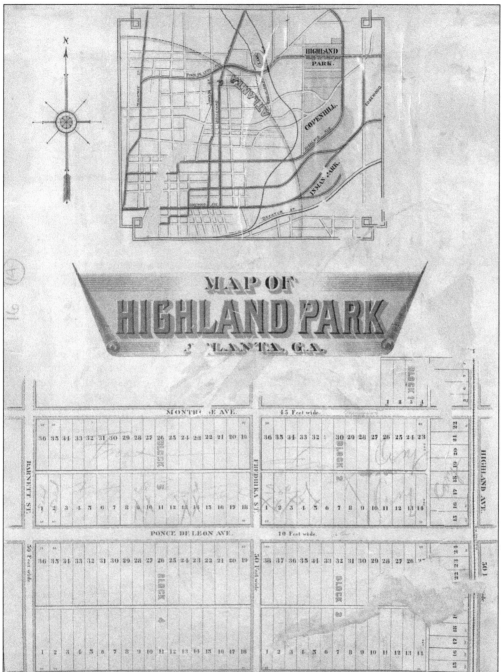

The area's first suburban development, Highland Park, was built on farmlands along Ponce de Leon between Highland and Barnett Street. Lots were offered in May 1893 for $1,000 each, with enticements for the first buyers. The subdivision was still growing in 1902 when 65 additional lots to the north were added on St. Charles and Greenwood Avenues. As the map shows, the trolley passed along Highland Avenue; the Ponce trolley line had not been extended east of Ponce de Leon Park. The Atlanta city limits did not include this area until 1909. (Courtesy of Kenan Research Center at the Atlanta History Center.)

Benjamin R. Padgett Sr. (shown in both photographs) followed his father, Hardy, in a career of construction and development. The Padgetts were among the first architectural and building contractors in Atlanta and were responsible for much of the development of the Highland Park subdivision. Main Hall, the original building on the Agnes Scott College campus, was another of their projects. Leila Ross Wilburn, a renowned female architect in the early 1900s, apprenticed under the Padgetts. Mrs. Ben R. Padgett Sr. (shown below) was very active at the Ponce de Leon Baptist Church and was honored as the "church mother" in 1932. (Courtesy of Julia Wynne.)

The Beautiful "Highland View"

SUB-DIVISION OF THE ATLANTA DEVELOPMENT COM-
PANY'S PROPERTY of over 40 acres. Situated in the very best
residential section of Atlanta, Ga.—on the North Side—with Ansley Park on its left and Druid Hills on its right.

Two street car lines. All city improvements. Schools
and churches. All lots sold with restrictions.

It is the "High-Class" residence section of Atlanta.

Adelaide Adair, G.B.'s widow, sold land just north of Highland Park and southwest of the main Highland-Virginia intersection to the Atlanta Development Company, which in 1911 created the Highland View subdivision. It featured 40 lots, each 50 by 250 feet, costing $1,400 to $1,700 each. This Atlanta Development Company advertisement indicates the subdivision was served by two streetcar lines and had enhanced city improvements. To emphasize the exclusivity of the subdivision, the lots were sold with restrictions. (Courtesy of Kathryn King-Metters, Rob Glancy, Kenan Research Center at the Atlanta History Center.)

Atkins Park was designed as a speculative residential development by Edwin Wiley Grove (below, left), a businessman based in St. Louis, Missouri. A Tennessee native, Grove made his fortune with his Paris Medicine Company, which he founded in 1878. He marketed Grove's Tasteless Chill Tonic, a lemon-flavored quinine drink that reduced the symptoms of malaria. A millionaire by the age of 44, he was involved in a variety of philanthropic causes and business ventures, including the Grove Park Inn in Asheville, North Carolina. In 1902, his St. Louis Investment Company began to acquire the land north of Ponce de Leon Avenue and east of Highland Avenue; the subdivision was platted in 1912. (Above, courtesy of Kenan Research Center at the Atlanta History Center, Atkins Park Garden Club; below, both courtesy of Grove Park Inn and Grovewood Gallery.)

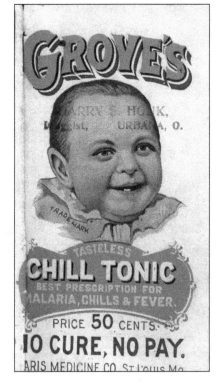

Atkins Park was originally called St. Louis Park, but Grove renamed it in honor of his mentor, Col. John DeWitt Clinton Atkins (right) of Paris, Tennessee. A farmer, Colonel Atkins was also a member of the Confederate Provisional Congress during the Civil War and later the US House of Representatives. President Cleveland appointed Atkins commissioner of Indian Affairs in 1885; he died in 1908. (Courtesy of Library of Congress: cwpbh03957 Brady.)

Fred Seely (left), who married Grove's only daughter, oversaw the development ventures. He worked with John Oscar Mills, who was the landscape and construction supervisor. Seely gained notoriety for his business savvy and commitment to social causes. In 1906, he founded the *Atlanta Georgian* newspaper to expose chain-gang labor practices in Georgia and other issues. (Courtesy of Grove Park Inn, Grovewood Gallery.)

Grove and Seely created a park-like setting with tree-lined streets, stone curbs, and wide sidewalks. The stone gates at both ends of St. Augustine Place and St. Charles Place and the western end of St. Louis Place conveyed a sense of exclusivity. The columns frame the women of the Atkins Park Garden Club in this 1935 photograph. (Courtesy of Kenan Research Center at the Atlanta History Center, Atkins Park Garden Club.)

Atkins Park was designed as an orderly grid. Servants were not permitted in front of the homes; they were restricted to alleys between the rear property lines. A sidewalk through the middle of the subdivision (seen at left), now called Malcolm's Way, paralleled Highland Avenue and allowed quicker access to the Ponce trolley. (Courtesy of Kenan Research Center at the Atlanta History Center, Atkins Park Garden Club.)

In 1912, pharmacist John B. Daniel (right) owned the property bounded by St. Charles Avenue, Ponce de Leon Avenue, Highland Avenue, and Frederica Street. After his death, his nephew Lucian Lamar Knight (below) inherited the land and divided it into 81 lots. In 1916, Knight built the Colonnade Apartments at 828–832 Highland Avenue; the Colonnades were two luxury three-story buildings with 12 apartments each. Best known as a historian and prominent journalist and as literary editor for the *Atlanta Constitution*, Knight was also an orator, like his cousin Henry Grady. Knight often served as master of ceremonies for various events. Later, he was the founder and first director of the Georgia Archives. (Courtesy of State of Georgia Archives, Office of Secretary of State.)

In March 1922, Bernard Wildauer, a dentist, constructed a beautiful apartment complex—The St. Charles—at what is now 1026 St. Charles Avenue. The builder was O.J. Southwell; the complex of 16 apartments (each with five or six rooms) cost $100,000, a fortune at the time. The St. Charles offered a touch of class and style to the many businessmen moving to Atlanta and was considered one of the area's nicer apartment buildings. Wildauer's wife, Mollie, lived there until she died in 1963. The building is now condominiums; the design and exterior have remained effectively unchanged. (Courtesy of Ellen Dracos Lemming.)

In 1914, the Ford Motor Company made the decision to concentrate its sales, service, administration, assembly, and shipping operations for four southern states in Atlanta. Its assembly plant at what is now 699 Ponce de Leon Avenue was one of the earliest built in the southeast and signaled the beginning of automobile manufacturing in Atlanta. At its peak, Ford sold an annual average of 22,000 vehicles, including the Model T (1915 to 1927), Model A (1927 to 1932), and V-8 (1932 to 1937). This building remained the headquarters of Ford's southeastern operations from 1915 until 1942, when it was sold to the US War Department. During the Vietnam War, it was an induction center for those entering the military and was the site of several antiwar protests. The four-story, rectangular building, trimmed with terra cotta and colored tile, is an outstanding example of early 20th-century commercial and industrial architecture in Atlanta. (Courtesy of the Collections of The Henry Ford, P.833.41166/THF100915.)

Ernest G. Beaudry (left) was among the most well-known residents of Atkins Park. He founded the Beaudry Ford Motor Company in 1916. He and his family lived at 1160 St. Augustine Place, originally 74 St. Augustine Place, from 1919 until 1930. (Courtesy of Special Collections and Archives, Georgia State University Library.)

Sears, Roebuck and Co. bought the former Ponce de Leon Springs in 1925 and announced it would build a giant retail store and mail-order house. Sears paid $200,000 for the 16-acre site, and the city agreed to extend North Avenue to the new building. The springs became an artesian well that served the plant. In August 1926, Sears opened the first phase of the mammoth facility, which became its southeastern regional headquarters. On the first day, it reported 30,000 visitors—the largest opening day at that point in Sears history—and 4,000 mail orders. It carried 35,000 items and employed 1,500 people. The building expanded several times over the following decades. By 1960, the facility totaled two million square feet. (Above, courtesy of The Kenan Research Center at Atlanta History Center; below, courtesy of Special Collections and Archives, Georgia State University Library.)

The original Ponce Park stadium was built in 1907. It burned in 1923 and was rebuilt by Rell Jackson Spiller, who renamed it Spiller Field. Spiller, an affluent concessionaire who lived on St. Charles Place, was the team's sole owner until 1932, when he sold it to The Coca-Cola Company. Renamed Ponce de Leon Park, it was home to the Atlanta Crackers. The club flourished during the minor-league baseball boom after World War II. By the late 1950s attendance had dwindled, a decline often attributed to television. Other than a 1949 exhibition game featuring Jackie Robinson and the Brooklyn Dodgers, the club and park were segregated until the early 1960s. Black fans sat in separate stands on the right and left field lines. (Both, courtesy of Special Collections and Archives, Georgia State University Library.)

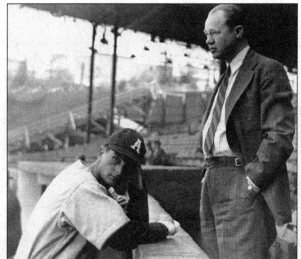

Earl Mann (above left) with Crackers player Paul Richards and (above right) with Mae West bought the Crackers from Coca-Cola in 1947. His son, Oreon (below, center), took the bus from school to the ballpark to be the team's batboy. Oreon remembers Crackers' hitting legend Bob Montag smashing a titanic home run into the coal car of a train on the tracks above right field. The train operator who found the smudged ball returned it later, declaring it the "longest home run ever, going about 518 miles." The train tracks are now part of the Atlanta BeltLine. Oreon became a loyal customer of George's Restaurant. (Courtesy of Oreon Mann.)

John H. Whisenant, a real estate businessman from Habersham County, built this large home in 1910 at 885 Highland Avenue. As they built their home, John and his wife Lula rented at 916 Highland Avenue. According to the 1920 census, they lived at 885 Highland Avenue with their son, brother, and six other boarders. A small building was erected behind the larger home, where their servants lived. (Courtesy of Jill Marber.)

The Virginia Avenue subdivision (the south side of Virginia Avenue, and north side of Virginia Circle between Todd Road and Barnett Street) attracted many doctors, attorneys, and businessmen. Dr. Rupert Fike bought 931 Virginia Avenue after returning from studying radiation therapy at the Curie Institute in France. He treated cancer patients throughout the Southeast. From 1923 to 1950, the home was a gathering place for members of Atlanta's medical community. One of the first collegiate booster clubs, IPTAY of Clemson University, was formed there in 1933. Ralph McGill, Sen. Richard Russell, and Margaret Mitchell attended the Fikes' 25th wedding anniversary at the home. On the night of the premiere of *Gone with the Wind* in 1939, a band played in the home after the official dance at the municipal auditorium. (Courtesy of Rupert Fike III, Rosa Arriaga.)

Atlanta, Ga.
Jan. 29, 1938

Dear Dr. and Mrs. Fike:
John and I thank you so much for your invitation for Sunday, February sixth. If we are in town next week we will be happy to come.
cordially,
Peggy Mitchell Marsh

The growing population in the area required additional city infrastructure. Atlanta Fire Station #19 was built in 1925 at the corner of Highland and Los Angeles Avenues. Its bungalow style, with Italianate details, reflects the neighborhood's architecture. The city engineer, C.E. Kauffman, built the station as a joint effort between the City of Atlanta and Fulton County. Station #19 is Atlanta's oldest continuously operating fire station. An antique 1925 American LaFrance fire engine that represents the truck used at Station #19 in the early years is displayed in the back of the station. (Courtesy of Kenan Research Center at the Atlanta History Center.)

Aaron Valentine, fire captain at Station #19, and his men, were among those who fought the blaze at the Winecoff Hotel on December 7, 1946. The hotel, designed and built in 1913 in downtown Atlanta, had no sprinklers, fire escapes, or alarm systems. In this tragedy, 119 people lost their lives, some leaping from windows. Captain Valentine wept when he went home that night; it was the only time his daughter Laurie ever saw him cry. (Right, courtesy Jim Zwald; below, courtesy of Georgia Archives, Vanishing Georgia Collection, Office of Secretary of State.)

Rapid transit and automobiles spurred the extension of the residential districts and brought previously distant points within range of the heart of the city. Many of Atlanta's business and professional men began the inner-city exodus toward suburbia. This c. 1923 photograph of the intersection of Highland and Virginia Avenues looks east toward the site of the future extension of Virginia Avenue. The east side of Highland Avenue was lined with homes prior to the expansion of the commercial district. (Courtesy of Tom Catron.)

Ben R. Padgett Jr. (left) continued the family tradition in development as manager of L.W. Rogers Realty. In 1923, he established the Virginia Highlands subdivision, which extended Virginia Avenue east to Rosedale Road and Hudson Drive over to Highland Avenue. (Courtesy of Tom Catron.)

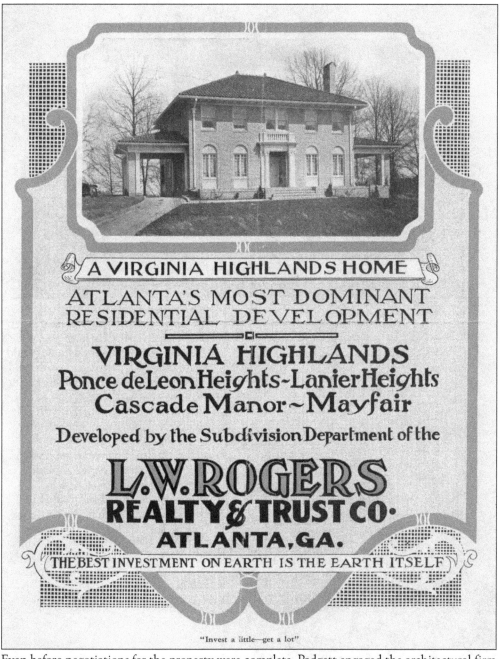

Even before negotiations for the property were complete, Padgett engaged the architectural firm of Daniel & Beutell to draw up plans for his own home (currently 1060 Virginia Avenue), which was the first in the Virginia Highlands subdivision. The house is pictured here on his firm's advertisement and on the preceeding page at right in the top image. The home cost approximately $25,000, making it significantly more expensive than most houses in the neighborhood. Many of the 120 lots were sold by the time the sale was officially announced. Ben's brother Hardy also built a house in the neighborhood on Hudson Drive. (Courtesy of Tom Catron.)

Above, Ben Padgett Jr. is surrounded by his family around 1923, including twin A.B. Padgett, who was later honored with the Atlanta Shining Light Award. May Andrews Padgett (left), with her older brother Benjamin Padgett III, in 1910, was the first child born in Ansley Park, which she claimed was "why she had been going around in circles her whole life." When her family moved to the Virginia Highlands subdivision, her father built her a special music room. Padgett and his wife were charter members of the Druid Hills Baptist Church, then at the corner of Greenwood and Highland Avenues. In 1925, the Padgetts moved to Tampa and lost their fortune in the real estate bust. (Courtesy of Tom Catron.)

Atlanta's schools were segregated by gender and race. White males attended Boys High School and Tech High, located on Charles Allen Avenue (then Parkway Drive). In 1947, the schools—historically intense academic and athletic rivals—merged with Girls High into co-educational Henry W. Grady High School (above), named for the *Atlanta Constitution* editor. The yearbook (the *Orator*) and newspaper (the *Southerner*) both honor Grady's career. The school's neoclassical design was the work of architect Philip Schutze. Inman School (right), originally the Virginia Avenue School, was built as an elementary school in 1923. Named after the 19th-century cotton merchant and advocate of education Samuel Inman, it was built to serve 630 students. More than 1,000 children from the growing area enrolled on the first day. (Above, courtesy of Kenan Research Center at the Atlanta History Center; right, courtesy of Atlanta Fulton County Library, Special Collections.)

Atlanta's first condominiums were built at 982 Virginia Avenue in 1921 by Dewald Cohen, who had seen multi-unit occupant-owned buildings while at a Shriner's convention in Indianapolis. The building had four homes; the Cohens lived in Unit No. 3 with their daughter Natalie, who became a tennis champion and may have planted the large poplar now in front of the building. (Courtesy of Ellen Dracos Lemming.)

Stella Steinheimer Bauer and her husband, Henry, lived in a bottom unit of the condos in the 1930s. Lena Fox, Alfred Uhry's grandmother, was a good friend of Stella's and a frequent visitor to the Bauer home. The character of Miss Daisy in Uhry's award-winning play *Driving Miss Daisy* may have been based on Lena. (Courtesy of Judith Cohen.)

The Jacobsen family lived at 982 Virginia Avenue above the Bauers. Bert Jacobsen, their younger son, went into showbusiness. He changed his last name to Parks and became an actor, singer, and announcer for radio and television. He is best known as the longtime host of the Miss America Pageant from 1955 to 1979. Before he moved to New York at age 19, Parks may have been offered his first broadcasting job at Atlanta's WGST Radio by his neighbor G.B. Adair Jr. Parks's classic rendition of the song "There She Is, Miss America" is still used each year in the Miss America Pageant as the new reigning titleholder walks down the runway. (Courtesy of Special Collections and Archives, Georgia State University Library.)

A variety of architectural styles and types exist throughout the various subdivisions in the neighborhood. The bungalow style was a response to the increasing need for modest single-family homes and was popular between 1900 and 1930. Bungalows are typically long and low with an irregular floor plan. Porches are common, as are low-pitched roofs with wide overhangs. The typical middle class housewife of the era would not have had live-in domestic servants. She did much of the housework and also watched the children herself. Such activities were made easier by having kitchens integrated into the main house, within easy sight of the common areas and backyard. These bungalows at 751 Virginia Circle (photographed in the 1940s) and 379 Cooledge Avenue, are excellent examples. (Above, courtesy of Special Collections and Archives, Georgia State University; below, courtesy of Ellen Dracos Lemming.)

Between 1915 and 1925, the North Boulevard Park Development Company developed the area from Park Drive south to Cooledge Avenue as North Boulevard Park. Most of the lots were sold by 1921. The success of that venture led to the development of Brookridge subdivision to the east, later known as Orme Park. This photograph of 663 Park Drive was found in a time capsule when the house was remodeled. (Courtesy of Maria Isabel LeBlanc.)

Clear Creek and the busy railway tracks were obstacles to accessing Piedmont Park and the neighborhoods to the west. In 1916, the development company, the city, and the Southern Railway built a bridge leading into the park over the tracks at Park Drive. The park's internal roads served as shortcuts from Boulevard (later Monroe Drive) to Piedmont Road and 14th Street until the late 1970s, when all through traffic was banned. (Courtesy of Ellen Dracos Lemming.)

The North Boulevard Park subdivision attracted many professionals and managers, including Lambdin Kay, who lived at 673 Cresthill Avenue. Kay was the station master at WSB Radio, where his on-air personality was "The Voice of the South." He was the co- founder of the Peabody Awards for excellence in radio broadcasting, modeled after the Pulitzer Prizes. Kay is also known for creating NBC's famous three-note tune. Responding to a WSB listener's request for a station break signal, Kay created the on-air tones with a xylophone to notify listeners that the program was live. When WSB became an affiliate of NBC in 1927, the concept was adopted nationwide. (Courtesy of Library of Congress: ggbain36879 and Cox Media Group.)

"The Seven Fifty," a 200-unit luxury apartment building designed by architect G. Lloyd Preacher, was built in 1925 on the corner of Highland and Ponce de Leon Avenues by the real estate firm owned by Asa G. Candler Jr., son of the founder of The Coca-Cola Company. The building features a stylized Mediterranean top with arched windows. Candler's real-estate development firm occupied the building's top floor, and he maintained a nine-room suite for his family to use. During the Depression, the building was converted to a commercial hotel, with 400 units that offered inexpensive rates. Later renamed the Briarcliff Hotel, it deteriorated after Candler's death. (Above, courtesy of Robin Davis; below, courtesy of Ellen Dracos Lemming.)

Charles Kliros (left) was born in 1902 in Tripoli, in the Peloponnese region of Greece and came to the United States at age 13 by boat. Upon the death of his older brother, who had immigrated earlier, Charles assumed the responsibility of an eldest son. He worked multiple jobs and sent money monthly to his family in Greece. In 1929, Charles opened his first Majestic Diner on Peachtree Road, followed by another on Ponce de Leon Avenue in 1936. Open 24 hours a day, the Majestic attracted professionals moving into the area. It offered a wide variety of American food, including what he termed a "famously good cheeseburger." Over the years, the Majestic provided jobs for relatives who followed Charlie to the country. (Left, courtesy of Mike Andriola and Helen Cassandras; below, courtesy of Robin Davis.)

The community attracted many immigrants, particularly Greek, Middle Eastern, and Italian. The sidewalks and local shops reminded many of their native countries. Voula Papadopoulos, from Greece, married Leonard "Andy" Andriola, a first-generation Italian American. She is shown here on her wedding day leaving for the church from her home at Highland and Virginia. They continued to celebrate their ethnic heritage as they built their life together. (Courtesy of Mike Andriola.)

Nass Almeleh, a Jewish merchant born in 1885 in Greece, arrived in Atlanta in 1928. He operated Nass Shoe Repair near Atkins Park for 55 years. He lived on Rosedale, walking to the store daily. His secret to a long life was drinking two glasses of warm water with lemon at breakfast, one Budweiser—"it had to be Budweiser!"—for lunch, and a cocktail before dinner. (Courtesy of Martha Perlmutter.)

In 1928, John and Lucy Crenshaw and their children moved to 740 Virginia Circle. Then part of the Virginia Hills subdivision, covenants forbade property being "sold, leased, or rented to Persons of Jewish or African Descent." In the 1930s, a Jewish woman planned to move to Virginia Circle. Uneasy neighbors approached John Crenshaw (below), an attorney, for his opinion. He asked, "Does she have money to buy the house? If so, let her live there." After she moved in, the Crenshaws walked up the street to welcome her with a meal. Their pleased new neighbor invited them inside, but John insisted that they eat on the lawn to make it plain to other neighbors that she was welcome into the community. (Courtesy of Lucy Crenshaw Kelley.)

Dr. Leila Daughtry-Denmark, MD, born in 1898 in Portal, Georgia, was the third female to graduate from the Medical College of Georgia. She practiced pediatric medicine in the neighborhood from 1931 to 1949 and was the go-to person for most of the mothers. Pictured here in 1936 with her daughter Mary, she believed that a mother should personally raise her children. Mary was always by her side as she cared for her patients. She conducted research on the diagnosis, treatment, and immunization of whooping cough and received multiple awards and accolades throughout her 70 years of practice. She practiced from her home at 1051 Hudson Drive; the living room served as the waiting room. Dr. Denmark did not keep an appointment schedule, but would peek her head out of the examination room, saying, "Now which one is my next little angel?" In 2011, she was 113 years old and one of the oldest people on the planet. (Courtesy of Mary Denmark Hutcherson.)

Mary Denmark Hutcherson grew up at 1051 Hudson Drive in the 1930s. She played with her girlfriends Ann Tinkler, daughter of the Associate Reform Presbyterian Church minister, and Bootsie Holzman. Sidewalks made for great roller-skating and kids played outside with little supervision. They would run to see the fire truck go by, loved the dime store, and enjoyed milkshakes at Mrs. Georgia's dairy on Highland Avenue. (Courtesy of Mary Denmark Hutcherson.)

Mary attended Inman from kindergarten through sixth grade and O'Keefe (now on the Georgia Tech campus) for middle school. After that, she went to Girls High in Grant Park for 10th and 11th grade and then graduated from Grady High in 1948 in the school's first co-ed class. (Courtesy of Mary Denmark Hutcherson, Clyde Daughters.)

The Church of Our Saviour was founded in 1924 by former congregants of the Church of the Epiphany in Little Five Points. Key support from the Episcopal Diocese was provided by the Right Reverend Judah Mikell and the Reverend George Gasque (below). The congregation rented premises for one year before moving in 1925 to its current location opposite Fire Station #19. The church was consecrated in 1944 and expanded in the 1950s, when the original building's wooden walls (shown at right) were covered by brick and folded into the new structure. All the facilities are named in honor of former assistant clergy. The Church of Our Saviour has always celebrated an Episcopal "high church" liturgy. Father John Bolton, who became priest-in-charge in 2006, led a movement toward broader congregational involvement in community and social issues. (Both, courtesy of The Church of Our Saviour.)

The Associate Reformed Presbyterian Church, organized downtown in 1890, moved to 1001 Highland Avenue in 1923. The church building was constructed for an estimated $62,000 and the manse for over $9,000, including the lot on Hudson. The congregation could not maintain the loan payments during the Depression, and for several years they struggled to pay the interest. Dr. Tom McDill served the church from 1946 to 1951, when the congregation experienced tremendous growth in membership and service. In 1973, the congregation relocated to Stone Mountain. The building was later sold to the YWCA and continues to be a center for neighborhood activity. Note the trolley lines on Highland Avenue (above). (Above, courtesy of Special Collections and Archives, Georgia State University Library; below, courtesy of Highlands Presbyterian Church and Emilie Wingfield.)

Led by Rabbi Tobias Geffen, the Shearith Israel Synagogue moved in 1958 from Washington Street to University Drive in Morningside, becoming the first synagogue in DeKalb County. The synagogue, whose name means "Remnant of Israel," served the large Jewish population that moved to the area from south of the Georgia State Capitol. Baptist minister and educator Charles Fowler built the structure in 1917 to house Lanier University. He envisioned a campus of buildings that resembled famous Southern mansions, but only one—a copy of the Curtis-Lee Mansion—was built before the university failed in the early 1940s. In a story that could not be made up, the Ku Klux Klan purchased the school and property and sold it to Jewish residents one year later for what became the synagogue. (Right, courtesy of Mary Alyce Ware; below, courtesy of Congregation Shearith Israel.)

The Virginia Avenue Baptist Church congregation (below) began meeting in 1923 in a small white structure built by charter member T.A. Hallman on the corner of Virginia Avenue and Ponce de Leon Place. Sunday school classrooms, the two extended structures seen in the photograph above (looking southeast with Ponce de Leon Place in the foreground), were added to the original frame building. The stone wall and steps are still used today. The church was an important neighborhood center into the 1960s. (Both, courtesy of Virginia-Highland Church.)

The current sanctuary for the Virginia Avenue Baptist Church was built in 1950. Shown above is the groundbreaking ceremony, after the pastor blessed the land. Inman School is visible behind the congregation. The church was renamed the Virginia-Highland Baptist Church in 1992 to reflect its connection to the community. The church's governing body, the Southern Baptist Convention, steadily became more conservative in the 1980s; the neighborhood and the congregation became more progressive. In the mid-1990s, the Convention pressured the congregation to alter its practice of ordaining women. It opposed the church's 1993 decision to label itself an "inclusive congregation that welcomed lesbian, gay, bisexual, and transgender members." By 2002, all formal affiliations with the Southern Baptist and Georgia Baptist Conventions had ended. The congregation today is known as Virginia-Highland Church and continues its progressive witness as a member of the United Church of Christ and the Alliance of Baptists. (Courtesy of Virginia-Highland Church.)

Brothers Moe and Joe Krinsky returned from World War II and opened Moe's and Joe's in 1947. Still going strong a half-century later, the bar has attracted some distinctive patrons, including a regular with a Rolls Royce who offered the brothers the car for a year's worth of free beer. The men quickly agreed, and Moe and Joe (standing in back) provided play money for unlimited beer. (Courtesy of Howard Krinsky, Tracy Crowley.)

Horace McKennie served at Moe's and Joe's for 52 years, each day wearing his bowtie, suspenders, and formal jacket. Ever the consummate gentleman, he loved to tell jokes, though never a dirty one with ladies present. He considered Moe's and Joe's a classy community bar and would never tolerate gambling or displays of affection he deemed inappropriate. (Courtesy of Tracy Crowley, Jim Perman.)

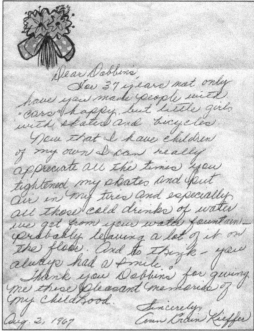

Dear Dobbins,

For 37 years not only have you made people with "cars" happy, but little girls with skates and bicycles.

Now that I have children of my own I can really appreciate all the times you tightened my skates and put air in my tires and especially all those cold drinks of water we got from your water fountain—probably leaving a lot of it on the floor. And to think - you always had a smile.

Thank you Dobbins for giving me these pleasant memories of my childhood.

Sincerely,
Ann Erwin Kieffer

Aug. 2, 1967

Hoke Dobbins Herrington (above) began working at the Standard Oil filling station on the southeast corner of Highland and Virginia Avenues in 1928 at age 17; several years later, he bought the business. He was not drafted in World War II because his business was deemed vital. After the war, he allowed customers to sign a promissory "ticket" for future payment; when he died, his family found stacks of unpaid tickets. Over the years, Herrington slowly acquired more and more property, ultimately owning more than 11 different parcels. Known for his hard work ethic and generous outlook, he drew a following of neighborhood children. His family continues to live in the community and manage the property, though it is no longer a filling station. (Courtesy of Lynn DeWitt.)

Helen and Jim Lee moved from Berkeley, California, with their first child in 1946 to be near his parents. They initially lived with seven adults and one child in a two-bedroom bungalow on Los Angeles Avenue. In 1951, they opened a photography studio at 1001 Highland Avenue, next to Herrington's Filling Station. In 1961, they moved their home and studio to 1164 North Highland Avenue (shown below with family members in front), which they bought for $17,000 and spent $13,000 remodeling. For 35 years, they photographed weddings, parties, bar and bat mitzvahs, and notable citizens of the community, including transvestite Diamond Lil. (Courtesy of Helen Lee.)

As more families purchased cars, other filling stations opened along Highland Avenue. In 1931, brothers Doyle A. and Bell J. Langford opened a service station at the corner of Highland and Drewry Street (above). Originally called Woco-Pep, the station later became Pure Oil Company and later Union Oil Company. The current building was constructed in 1939 and remained a filling station for over 50 years. There was a small rose garden on the Drewry side of the station for the neighbors. The building has since been converted into a restaurant. The photograph below shows another neighborhood filling station at the southeast corner of Amsterdam and Highland Avenues. (Above, courtesy of Justin Haynie and J.R. Marchman; below, courtesy of Special Collections and Archives, Georgia State University Library.)

The 1949 aerial photograph below shows (in the upper left corner) the first commercial building at the intersection of Amsterdam Avenue (east–west) and Highland Avenue (north–south) in the intersection's southwest corner. The structure sits on a lot sold in the 1930s by the Cheshires, whose family home is barely visible through the trees. Among the site's first business owners were brothers Leonard (left) and Irwin Greenbaum, immigrants from Latvia, who started a small, full-service grocery. Their sister Betty described the area as "not really bustling, but Highland was an active thoroughfare with the trolley running by." After Prohibition, the brothers wanted to sell liquor, but the proximity of the Lutheran Church forced them to find a new location. They opened Green's Liquor on Ponce de Leon Avenue and eventually Tower Liquor on Piedmont. (Left, courtesy of Jerry Greenbaum; below, courtesy of Georgia State University Library.)

Louis Vrono operated Vrono's Supermarket at the corner of Highland and Amsterdam Avenues in the early 1940s. When his son Harold (below, walking) returned from World War II, they expanded further south on Highland Avenue. A separate building was erected in the late 1940s at 1186 Highland, with a parking lot between the two commercial centers. Vrono's Supermarket moved to the new location (above). The supermarket was well known for its promotions, sometimes featuring ponies and cows. A cow once escaped up Bellevue Drive and created a great chase scene. A post office was added in 1960. It was originally a large carrier distribution facility where the delivery trucks parked in back and was later downsized. Some of its space was converted to restaurant and retail space. (Courtesy of Harold Vrono.)

Atkins Park Pharmacy was built in 1914 at the corner of Highland and St. Charles Avenues. It became Cox & Baucom in the 1930s. The soda fountains of the era were neighborhood hangouts that provided gathering spaces for citizens, politicians, and teenagers. Jack Fleeman started as a curb boy, running medicine, food, and other sundries to waiting motorists. He took over the business in the late 1940s and renamed it Fleeman's Pharmacy. In its heyday, this famous pharmacy and soda fountain was a hot spot that sold chocolate, lime, and even celery-flavored Coca-Cola. Jack Fleeman met his wife in the pharmacy. The building's renowned vintage-style Coca-Cola mural was created in 1982, in the style of an 1890s advertisement. The original windows were bricked for advertisements like this one; they have since been reopened. (Courtesy of Jackie Fleeman Gramatas; artist Jeanne Mack.)

Atkins Park Tavern is the oldest continuously licensed bar establishment in Atlanta. The building was built in 1910 as a home. In 1922, the structure was raised 20 feet, and the H.L. McHan family created a deli (now a bar) and retail space (now a restaurant) on the first floor. A stairway between the deli and retail space led to the second floor, where the family continued to live. The bar's reputation led some parents to demand that their children walk to the opposite side of the street when going to the theater next door at night. (Courtesy of Warren Bruno, Sandra Spoon.)

Atlanta's population grew from 154,000 in 1910 to nearly 200,000 in 1920. Many middle-class families acquired automobiles, and industrial and commercial employers were hiring along the Ponce de Leon corridor. In response, more multifamily housing was built, particularly in the southern portion of the neighborhood. Many employees of the Ford Motor Company assembly plant and the Sears, Roebuck and Co. facility chose to live close to work. There were only two apartment buildings in the area in 1923; over the course of the next 15 years, 21 more were built. Pictured here are 974 Greenwood Avenue (above) and 1034 Virginia Avenue (below). (Courtesy of Special Collections and Archives, Georgia State University Library.)

Four

CATALYSTS OF CHANGE

The 1960s transformed intown neighborhoods. The decade began with school integration, which caused divisions but was welcomed by many. The community's existence was threatened when the Georgia Highway Department announced plans for a major highway (I-485) straight through northeast Atlanta. The homes shown above at Clemont Drive and Greencove Avenue (now greenspace east of Inman School) were among many bought and demolished. (Courtesy of Jennifer Chambers.)

Racial integration impacted the intown neighborhoods. In 1959, the names of several streets were changed at Ponce de Leon Avenue to differentiate the white sections to the north from the mostly black sections to the south. The street name of Boulevard north of Ponce de Leon Avenue was changed to Monroe Drive. Racial integration in Atlanta public schools began peacefully in 1961 at Grady High School, in front of the national news corps. White flight accelerated across Atlanta throughout the next two decades. To promote integration, C.W. Hill Elementary School (in the mostly-black Bedford Pine neighborhood just south of Ponce de Leon Avenue) was paired with Morningside Elementary School. All first-graders, second-graders, and third-graders attended Hill; fourth-graders, fifth-graders, and sixth-graders went to Morningside. This 1973 photograph taken at Hill shows children in front of a bus bound for Morningside. (Courtesy of Kenan Research Center at the Atlanta History Center.)

The specter of the highway depressed property values in the targeted neighborhoods and accelerated the exodus of many older residents. Many homes were converted into apartments; the new occupants were typically younger and often active in Atlanta's antiwar and counterculture movements. "The Strip" at the corner of Tenth and Peachtree was a center of counterculture. Piedmont Park was a popular gathering place for music and demonstrations. The Allman Brothers Band and the Grateful Dead often played there, always for free. Anti–Vietnam War protests became more common throughout the decade, and many activists lived in the community. (Above, courtesy of Tom Coffin; right, courtesy of Kenan Research Center at the Atlanta History Center.)

We hold these truths to be self-evident: That all men are created equal; that they are endowed by their Creator with certain unalienable rights; that among these are life, liberty, and the pursuit of happiness; that to secure these rights, governments are instituted among men, deriving their just powers from the consent of the governed; that whenever any form of government becomes destructive of these ends, it is the right of the people to alter or to abolish it, and to institute new government, laying its foundation on such principles, and organizing its powers in such form, as to them shall seem most likely to effect their safety and happiness.

Quoted from: Black Panthers 1967
Ho Chih Minh 1945
The 13 Colonies 1776

The Great Speckled Bird grew out of the antiwar movement at Emory University and became known nationwide as the region's countercultural voice. The city's civil rights, women's, labor, and gay movements were covered at the paper, which was hawked by a legion of street vendors. Published weekly from 1968 to 1976, *The Bird* endured a firebombing, several lawsuits, and constant police attention. The staff (below) worked for minimal—and sometimes no—pay. Many neighborhood residents, most notably Tom and Stephanie Coffin, contributed to the paper. *The Bird* made decisions in a collective and democratic fashion, but the central role of the Coffins was unmistakable. Both later became arborists; over the next 40 years they planted hundreds of trees in the neighborhood. (Left, courtesy of Jack White; below, courtesy of Tom Coffin.)

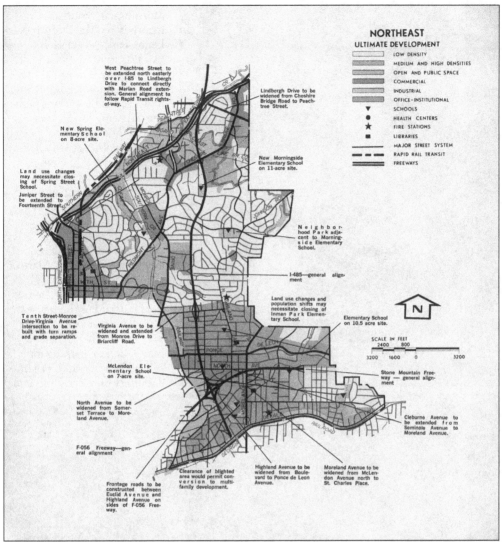

NORTHEAST
ULTIMATE DEVELOPMENT

LOW DENSITY
MEDIUM AND HIGH DENSITIES
OPEN AND PUBLIC SPACE
COMMERCIAL
INDUSTRIAL
OFFICE-INSTITUTIONAL
▼ SCHOOLS
● HEALTH CENTERS
★ FIRE STATIONS
■ LIBRARIES
——— MAJOR STREET SYSTEM
--- --- RAPID RAIL TRANSIT
═══ FREEWAYS

West Peachtree Street to be extended north easterly over I-85 to Lindbergh Drive to connect directly with Marian Road extension. General alignment to follow Rapid Transit rights-of-way.

Lindbergh Drive to be widened from Cheshire Bridge Road to Peachtree Street.

New Spring Elementary School on 8-acre site.

Land use changes may necessitate closing of Spring Street School.

Juniper Street to be extended to Fourteenth Street.

New Morningside Elementary School on 11-acre site.

Neighborhood Park adjacent to Morningside Elementary School.

I-485—general alignment

Land use changes and population shifts may necessitate closing of Inman Park Elementary School.

Elementary School on 10.5 acre site.

Tenth Street-Monroe Drive-Virginia Avenue intersection to be rebuilt with turn ramps and grade separation.

Virginia Avenue to be widened and extended from Monroe Drive to Briarcliff Road.

SCALE IN FEET
2400   800
3200   1600   0   3200

Stone Mountain Freeway — general alignment

McLendon Elementary School on 7-acre site.

North Avenue to be widened from Somerset Terrace to Moreland Avenue.

Cleburne Avenue to be extended from Seminole Avenue to Moreland Avenue.

F-056 Freeway—general alignment

Frontage roads to be constructed between Euclid Avenue and Highland Avenue on sides of F-056 Freeway.

Clearance of blighted area would permit conversion to multi-family development.

Highland Avenue to be widened from Boulevard to Ponce de Leon Avenue.

Moreland Avenue to be widened from McLendon Avenue north to St. Charles Place.

The outward migration of the 1950s and the decline of mass transit produced a generation of planners who viewed highways as the best way to move suburban commuters into downtown. In 1964, the Georgia Highway Department (GHD) proposed a new highway (I-485) to connect I-85 near Lindbergh Drive to a Stone Mountain Connector, also new. The I-485 highway was presented as a 6.27-mile limited-access highway with 8 to 10 lanes and speeds of 50 to 60 miles per hour. Four different routes were initially considered and a fifth was soon added. The roads would have crossed the Atlanta neighborhoods of Bass-Inman Park, Highland-Virginia, Morningside-Lenox Park, Martin Manor, and Piedmont Heights. The Federal Highway Administration approved the concept in October 1964, and authorized GHD to prepare preliminary plans. This 1970 City of Atlanta map shows I-485 with a bisected Orme Park, an interchange at Virginia Avenue, and Fourteenth Street extended through Piedmont Park to Monroe Drive. (Courtesy of Joseph Drolet, Department of Planning, Atlanta.)

Morningside residents incorporated the Morningside-Lenox Park Association (MLPA) in May 1965 to fight the highway. They filed suit in Fulton Superior Court in May 1966. The suit was denied the following June, as was its appeal. The highway appeared inevitable; MLPA switched to negotiating design changes. The Highway Department began condemning land and knocking down homes along Virginia Avenue. Traumatized residents observed their neighbors being displaced and homes destroyed. Martha Jernigan, who lived at 791 Virginia Avenue, watched from her yard as the houses at Arcadia Street and Virginia were razed. The current Inman School parking lot is behind Martha on the right. (Courtesy of Susan Kraham.)

Many of Morningside's recent arrivals were younger, bolder, and less conservative than their predecessors. A new MLPA leadership team, the so-called "blue jean elite," included Mary Davis, a recent Emory graduate who arrived with her family in 1967, as well as Barbara Ray, Virginia Gaddis, Adele Northrup, and Virginia Taylor. They led a political action committee that refused to concede. They and others went door to door with children in tow, raising more money for appeals and collecting petition signatures. Fundraising "Phooey Fairs" were held in Piedmont Park. Mary Davis stands here in front of a house on the corner of Virginia and Greencove Avenues, which was dilapidated after years of neglect by the owner, the Georgia Highway Department. She was elected to city council five times, serving the community from 1978 to 1998. (Courtesy of Mary Davis.)

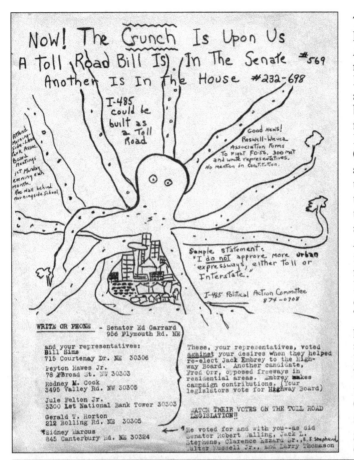

The newly-enacted National Environmental Protection Act (NEPA), signed in 1970, required an Environmental Impact Statement for parks and school districts impacted by federal funds. I-485's final route was adjacent to Inman School and crossed Orme Park. MLPA filed suit again in 1971, asking the federal court to require the Highway Department to prepare and submit such a study; the court agreed. Assessing environmental impacts was a subject for which the Highway Department had very limited expertise or enthusiasm. This requirement would be problematic for both I-485 and the Stone Mountain Freeway. The bottom bumper sticker below refers to Plains-native Jimmy Carter, who supported the road when he became governor in 1971. (Both, courtesy of Mary Davis.)

Atlanta, Yes! I-485, NO!

BUILD IT IN PLAINS

THE AMERICAN MUSIC SHOW   Cable Atlanta Channel 16 Mon/ Wed 10pm   Box 54472 Atlanta 30308

In the fall of 1971, a young assistant district attorney for Fulton County and new resident of Atlanta, Joseph Drolet (right and below, with Charles Longley), rented a home at 568 Park Drive. He was shocked that the Georgia Highway Department (GHD) was planning to build a highway directly through his quaint neighborhood. He began talking with neighbors about their opinions. A dormant neighborhood association, the Highland-Virginia Neighborhood Association (HVNA), had not had a meeting in years but its president had attended several GHD meetings, claiming that community residents were in favor of the proposed highway. This was not consistent with what Drolet had personally discovered from neighbors. (Courtesy of Joseph Drolet.)

State of Georgia

OFFICE OF SECRETARY OF STATE

I, Ben W. Fortson, Jr., Secretary of State of the State of Georgia, do hereby certify, that

based on a diligent search of the records on file in this office, I find that the name of the following proposed domestic corporation to wit

"VIRGINIA-HIGHLAND CIVIC ASSOCIATION, INC."

is not identical with or confusingly similar to the name of any other existing domestic or domesticated or foreign corporation registered in the records on file in this office or to the name of any other proposed domestic or domesticated, or foreign corporation as shown by a certificate of the Secretary of State heretofore issued and presently effective.

This certificate is in full force and effective for a period of 4 calendar months from date of issuance. After such period of time, this certificate is void.

In TESTIMONY WHEREOF, I have hereunto set my hand and affixed the seal of office, at the Capitol, in the City of Atlanta, this 22nd day of August, in the year of our Lord One Thousand Nine Hundred and Seventy Two and of the Independence of the United States of America the One Hundred and Ninety-seventh

Secretary of State, Ex-Officio Corporation
Commissioner of the State of Georgia

167

As Drolet collaborated with neighboring civic associations, like MLPA, he saw that his community needed a similar group to fight the highway. One immediate task was determining the specific boundaries of the neighborhoods. Drolet and MLPA president Mary Davis agreed that Amsterdam Avenue was a natural dividing line. On the west, he and the Uptown Neighborhood Association, representing what is now Midtown, settled on the railroad lines. Briarcliff Road, within Fulton County, provided the boundary on the east and Ponce de Leon Avenue on the south. In August 1972, the new association's steering committee chose the name "Virginia-Highland" to distinguish itself from the earlier "Highland-Virginia." In August 1972, the group was registered with the secretary of state. With that, the name of the community that we know today was born. (Courtesy of Joseph Drolet, VHCA.)

The first VHCA newsletter was published in August 1972 and explained the new association and the fight against the highway. A small group of people walked the streets to hand out the newsletters, which generated excellent attendance at the first meeting. Knowing that showcasing the area's residential renovations would raise both spirits and money, VHCA organized its first tour of homes later that year, featuring 13 renovated homes. While the legal battles continued, both VHCA and MLPA pressured local politicians to oppose the highway. In June 1973, the Atlanta Board of Aldermen voted 15-2 against the road; the proclamation was signed that evening at Manuel's Tavern by then-mayor Sam Massell. (Both, courtesy of Joseph Drolet.)

CELEBRATE!
A good old-fashioned Fourth of July.

Enjoy an art fair, a flea market, good food, singing and square dancing on Wednesday, July 4th, at Virginia Park 485, the cleared highway land in the 800 block of Virginia Avenue, NE. The occasion is the First Birthday of the Virginia-Highland Civic Association. The event will be held in conjunction with our clean-up of the land and will run from 10:00 A.M. to 10:00 P.M. Bring a rake or a hoe and a picnic lunch and come enjoy a good time with your neighbors.

Sponsored by

VIRGINIA-HIGHLAND CIVIC ASSOCIATION

In the summer of 1973, the VHCA steering committee organized a "sit-in" picnic and pig roast on the vacant land along Virginia Avenue. Assembling behind the Highway Department's "Do Not Trespass" signs, the crowd included political candidates running in the fall elections and drew the interest of the local media. The event continued through the decade. In 1977, it drew more than 4,000 people and featured a parade, a ringmaster, floats, bands, clowns, belly dancers, bagpipes, politicians, and the Fulton County Sheriff's team. (Left, courtesy of VHCA and Joseph Drolet; below, courtesy of Jackie Naylor.)

In the fall of 1973, Maynard Jackson put together a coalition of black and intown voters. He became the first African American elected to citywide office. He had campaigned opposing I-485, and his election signaled continued problems for the Highway Department. In the photograph above, Joseph Drolet (center, hands in pocket) and Charles Longley (far left) listen to Jackson campaign in Orme Park. The following year, the federal government rejected the Highway Department's new Environmental Impact Statement (EIS) on four different grounds, including its failure to consider alternative modes of transportation. The Highway Department ultimately dropped the road from its list of funding requests from the federal government, ending the 10-year fight over I-485. Over 900 parcels had been acquired and many homes had been demolished, but the neighborhood had survived. A significant percentage of its residents were young, active in politics, and socially diverse, and were schooled in the lessons of the Vietnam War, Watergate, and the I-485 fight. They were optimistic about their ability to make changes on many fronts. (Courtesy of Mary Davis.)

The Fourth of July festivities soon included a "Miss Tastefully Tacky Virginia-Highland Pageant" at Walter Mitty's, a bar on the site of today's Dark Horse Tavern. The lucky winner received a cardboard crown, a 20-pound bag of Vidalia onions, and other valued items. Sue Powers (left), the 1979 winner, poses in all of her glory with her fan. (Courtesy of Few Hembree.)

stone soup co-op membership card

This is to certify that the persons listed on the reverse of this card are entitled to full purchase privileges.

The Stone Soup Co-op at 996 Virginia Avenue was organized to purchase fresh vegetables and organic grains in bulk from the Farmer's Market; its members published a "back-to-the-earth, down-home" cookbook. The Co-op shared tasks and made decisions democratically. It had over 500 members at its peak. (Courtesy of Judy Beasley.)

Mayor Jackson also introduced "Herbie Curbies," which switched trash pickup from rear alleys to the street curb. These possum-proof containers greatly reduced trash on the ground, and the alleys behind many residences were no longer needed and became de facto additions to adjoining lots. Inspired Virginia-Highland residents staged "Herbies on Parade" competitions. Contestants dressed their cans in costume and marched through the neighborhood vying for awards, such as prettiest, ugliest, most patriotic, and most original. Jackson arrived in time to join a parade (right), which was followed by the Herbie 500, a race down Virginia Avenue with one person in the Herbie and one person pushing. Helmets and gloves were required. (Above, courtesy of Nancy Hamilton; right, courtesy of Few Hembree.)

Virginia-Highland's affordable housing and liberal atmosphere made it home to many progressive artists. The arts community of the day was smaller, passionate, and very supportive of its members, regardless of style. In 1972, a group revolving around photographer John McWilliams, a Georgia State University professor, started a grassroots artist cooperative called Nexus in a commercial space at the corner of Virginia Avenue and Rosedale Drive. The first photography gallery in the city, it later moved to Ralph McGill Boulevard in the old Forrest Elementary School location and became the Atlanta Contemporary Art Center. Nexus played a central role in the city's cultural landscape. (Courtesy of Chip Simone.)

George Beasley, professor at Georgia State University and an expert in the casting of iron sculpture, was chosen in 1977 to design the sculpture for the intersection of Virginia Avenue and Lanier Boulevard. The piece, *Bulwarks II*, was designed to convey the idea of water flowing through several abstract structures. Funded by the city's Bureau of Cultural Affairs, VHCA, and the National Endowment for the Arts, it was initially shown at the High Museum and installed in 1977. Judy Beasley is an accomplished potter; she crafted the ceremonial "Keys to the City" that were presented to Prince Charles during his 1977 visit. (Both, courtesy of Judy and George Beasley.)

Rufus Stansell was a legend in the community. A handyman for longtime property owner Hoke Herrington, Rufus lived in the basement apartment of 995 North Highland Avenue. Known for his wit—and his four marriages—he was a collector (who had 20 to 30 cuckoo clocks in his apartment!) and a folk artist who created whirligigs and more. Rufus was an aficionado of found art; for 20 years he added objets d'art, known as street art, to the chain-link fence next to his apartment building. When Rufus passed away of cancer in 2009, hundreds attended a memorial service in his backyard. (Courtesy of Kim Griffin.)

The young couples that arrived in the early 1970s soon needed childcare. Nancy Hamilton and Ann Roark devised an innovative solution, a babysitting co-op. "Babysitting Co-op" chits, earned by providing child-care and each worth a half hour, were soon a valuable currency. The Co-op created tremendous cohesion among the new parents and children who grew up together. As its membership grew, it held more of its own special events. Inevitably, some people accumulated more chits than others. One family traded a car—forever after the "chitmobile"—for another family's chit stash. (Courtesy of Nancy Hamilton, Shirley Hollberg, Jackie Naylor.)

In 1977, the Atlanta Pubic School system's final desegregation settlement was only five years old. Intown enrollments had dropped as families moved or sent their children to private schools. One response was the creation of the Council of Intown Neighborhoods and Schools (CINS). Primarily a general advocacy group for the viability and quality of public education, it also exchanged ideas and promoted best practices between the local schools. One of the initial founders, Nancy Hamilton, worked with Joe Martin, who became the school board's local representative. Morningside Elementary School's enrollment had dropped to 158 in 1976. After 25 years and multiple expansions, the overcrowding at Morningside required a new elementary school, Springdale Park Elementary, which was built in 2009. (Courtesy of Joe Martin and Nancy Hamilton.)

Five

COMMERCIAL REBIRTH

George Najour (far right) was Lebanese and had many friends in the neighborhood's ethnic community. He opened George's Deli (and bar) in 1961 at 1041 North Highland Avenue. The deli section sold sandwiches and Middle Eastern groceries and was replaced by a full kitchen in 1984. The bar has a large cadre of loyal customers, many of whom have been regulars for years. (Courtesy of G.G. Najour)

Najour's baseball abilities are reflected in the trophies that line the bar today. After his World War II service, he was offered a contract in the Dodgers farm system, but he signed instead with the Class D Newnan Browns of the Georgia-Alabama League. This allowed him to continue courting Mary, whom he married in 1950. Sports remain a large part of the conversation at George's. (Courtesy of G.G. Najour.)

Business was drawn back to the Virginia-Highland community in the early 1970s. Capo's Café (located at 992 Virginia Avenue, with the sign partly visible at left in the photograph) is one of the reasons more people returned. The small neighborhood café typically had waits of an hour or more, which gave visitors time to walk around the surrounding streets to visit other stores and explore the residential area. (Courtesy of Judy Beasley.)

The owners of Capo's were John (far right) and Linda Capozoli. John was attracted to the area by its sidewalks and pedestrian traffic; he saw a neighborhood waiting to happen. (Courtesy of Sheryl Meddin.)

In 1979, Sheryl Meddin and Bennett Frisch went out with their spouses and requested a table for dessert. The response was, "What!? For dessert only?" They opened The Dessert Place (a harbinger for future coffeehouses) three doors east of Capo's. Sheryl's husband, Stuart, was skeptical of the area's limited parking and unglamorous appearance, but Sheryl had a sixth sense about the area's potential. (Courtesy of Sheryl Meddin.)

The Dessert Place's excellent food and transformed interior (designed by Bill Johnson) soon made it a popular and chic destination. The Dessert Place had challenges getting zoning approvals from an adversarial city bureaucracy, an experience that foreshadowed those of other residents and commercial owners over the next few decades. Important assistance during this period was provided by local resident and architect Charles Longley (later deputy director of the City of Atlanta Bureau of Buildings), who helped navigate the variance process. Irene and Jamie Croft owned the northwest corner of the building at that time. Previously from California, Irene wanted to "transmogrify"—her West Coast term for "revitalize"— the neighborhood, emphasizing restaurants and boutique specialty stores instead of the practical retailers that provided basic services to local residents. (Both, courtesy of Sheryl Meddin.)

Stuart Meddin bought the northwest corner of the commercial district from Irene Croft in 1983. Meddin had grown up in Charleston, South Carolina, and appreciated the potential long-term value of historic properties. Meddin added the rear doors, windows, and patios to the building's rear façade and paved the back lot. Anticipating that smaller businesses and boutiques might create a unique and attractive business mix, he retained the original store fronts and chose not to rent to national franchises. The same philosophies made him a supporter of the Virginia-Highland Neighborhood Commercial District zoning ordinance in 2008. (Both, courtesy of Sheryl Meddin.)

Chris and Sharon Bagby (left) went to Georgia Tech and worked at King Hardware after graduating. They married in 1974 and lived at 914 Glen Arden Way, part of the neighborhood's burgeoning wave of young residents. They opened Highland Hardware in 1978 at 1034 North Highland Avenue. Like its southern Highland Avenue neighbor Intown Hardware (which opened in 1983), it attracted many residents who were renovating homes. Over the years, Highland Hardware became more and more specialized as a woodworking store. Nationally known craftsmen taught seminars that drew large crowds, including President Carter. Sharon Bagby is shown below making a sale to the president, who was accompanied by 12 Secret Service agents. By the early 21st century, the store had built a national reputation in woodworking. (Both, courtesy of Chris Bagby and Sharon Bagby.)

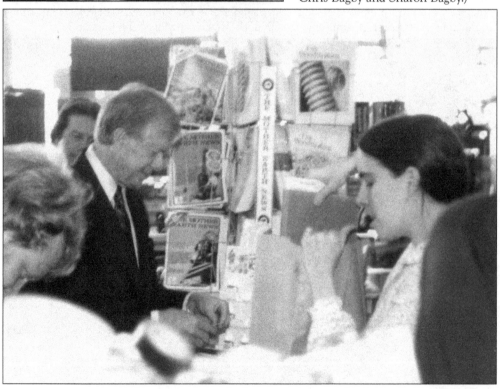

The old filling station lot at the corner of North Highland and Los Angeles Avenues was dirt and mud in the early 1970s. Chris Bagby mobilized local businesses to gravel the lot for improved parking. In 1981, the Bagbys bought the lot and the adjacent building at 1045 North Highland Avenue, previously housing Hopkins Drapery, from Robert Chambers (husband of Anne Cox Chambers) and moved Highland Hardware across the street. Architect Peter Hand, who designed several other local buildings, added a second-story mezzanine, large windows in the front, and an ornamental design that stylistically fit in with the neighborhood. The snowy image above (taken in the 1970s) depicts the building prior to its conversion. (Above, courtesy of Shirley Hollberg; below, courtesy of Chris Bagby and Sharon Bagby.)

Tom Murphy ran a gourmet cheese shop while in college and was known as "The Cheeseman." In 1980, he opened "Murphy's Round the Corner" in the basement of 1019 Los Angeles Avenue. He moved 13 years later to the southwest corner of Virginia and North Highland, previously occupied by an antique variety store. (Courtesy of Tom Murphy, Schroder Publishing.)

The sudden influx of coffee shops in the 1990s was an unmistakable sign of gentrification. At one point, there were five along North Highland Avenue. Among the first few were San Francisco Coffee House, Aurora, and Caribou Coffee (next to Highland Bagel). Caribou supplanted the once-popular Sunshine Center Laundromat, signaling the area's increasing number of owner-occupied homes and decreasing number of renters. (Courtesy of author.)

Six

FINDING A BALANCE

Each year in June, Summerfest brings the residents and businesses together for a weekend celebration that features a neighborhood dinner, parade, 5K road race, food and drinks, artists market, and music. Virginia Avenue is closed to cars; visitors arrive from across the Southeast. Though the traffic causes challenges for residents and businesses, the event generates funds for important neighborhood activities throughout the year. (Courtesy of author.)

Warren Bruno (center) purchased historic Atkins Park Restaurant and Bar in 1983, when it attracted a relatively lower-income clientele. He started Summerfest in 1984 as a block party with radio stations, live music, and local business sponsorship. Within six years, Summerfest expanded to all commercial nodes along North Highland; VHCA assumed leadership of the festival in 1990. Bruno remains a strong contributor to the festival and neighborhood. (Courtesy of Warren Bruno, Sandra Spoon.)

Aaron and Josephine Gross moved to Virginia-Highland in 1977. Aaron became a significant community leader, serving as president of VHCA, chair of Summerfest, and chair of NPU-F. After his death in 2004, the VHCA named its Community Service Award after Gross; it recognizes individuals who have made significant long-term contributions to the community. (Courtesy of Josephine Nunez-Gross.)

Long after the I-485 battle had been won, vacant lots and the foundations of a few homes remained along Virginia Avenue. Years of discussions about what to do with the land ended with a decision to build a park. The effort was led by a nonprofit park board and two other organizations, LAMP–AIDS and Volleyball Atlanta. The section of de Leon Place that originally extended to Virginia Avenue was closed and became part of the park. Homes that the GHD had taken down on the south side of Virginia are memorialized with small plaques bearing their original addresses on the granite columns that line the park along Virginia Avenue. (Courtesy of Jerry Bright.)

The park was named after John Howell, a gay rights activist and president of VHCA who died in 1988 from HIV complications. By this point, Virginia-Highland had a significant gay population. The park became one of the first in the country with an HIV component, creating an empathetic face associated with the tragic disease. (Courtesy of Jerry Bright.)

Jerry Bright (left) moved to Virginia-Highland from Chicago in the 1970s. He quickly got involved with other activists in the neighborhood and served as president of the board of John Howell Park. Rick Porter (right) oversaw the project management and facility installation in the park. Peter Frawley, chosen after an open bid process, was the landscape architect. The park was completed in 2000. (Courtesy of Jerry Bright.)

Many newspapers and literary journals started in Virginia-Highland, including *Creative Loafing,* the original *Atlanta Gazette, Southern Voice,* and *David Magazine. Creative Loafing* was published as a small entertainment and recreation weekly, "with a curious emphasis on television and league bowling." From 1973 to 1985, the weekly was housed at 1185 North Highland Avenue under the direction of Deborah and Elton "Chick" Eason. (Courtesy of Kenan Research Center at the Atlanta History Center.)

In 1998, Virginia-Highland mother Karen Page placed an article in a local paper seeking like-minded parents for social networking and community building. Those who responded formed the Virginia-Highland and Morningside Parents Association. This family resource has grown to a membership of over 600 families as of 2011 and has been a model for other parenting groups nationally. Karen Page and her son Alex are shown above. (Courtesy of Karen Page.)

Tragedy struck Virginia-Highland in 2003. A July thunderstorm approached suddenly as Lisa and Brad Cunard and their two children, Max and Owen, sat in traffic. A 100-year-old oak tree at 1072 North Highland Avenue fell onto their car. The firemen at Fire Station #19 ran to their assistance. Lisa and the two boys died instantly. Miraculously, Brad was physically unharmed. (Courtesy of Brad Cunard and Cynthia Gentry.)

Cynthia Gentry led the efforts to create a playground dedicated to the family. A two-level memorial garden and playground featured bronze reliefs of Lisa and the boys. Boy Scout Troop #17, which made the first donation of $1,000 from popcorn sales, volunteered to camp out overnight to ensure the playground equipment was safe during the installation phase. (Courtesy of Cynthia Gentry.)

More than 400 volunteers built the Cunard Memorial Playground in little over three months after the accident. Neighborhood teams worked in shifts preparing the land, installing the equipment, and landscaping. The memorial garden features three trees, one for each life lost, surrounded by flowers donated by local nurseries. The park is a testimony to what a community can achieve when inspired to help others. (Courtesy of Cynthia Gentry.)

An opening ceremony was held in March 2004. A special presentation was made to Brad Cunard in celebration of the memory of Lisa, Max, and Owen. The children of the Haygood Cherub Choir sang Max Cunard's favorite song. Included in the playscape is a play fire truck with #19 on it to thank the fire fighters who immediately came to the Cunards' assistance. (Courtesy of Cynthia Gentry.)

Individuals in the neighborhood continued the heritage of scrutinizing development. Residents were active in successful fights to save the Fox Theater in the 1970s and a second major highway struggle, the 1980s Presidential Parkway leading to the new Carter Center. Many neighborhood residents and NPU-F led a city-wide but ultimately unsuccessful effort to stop the Atlanta Botanical Gardens from building a parking deck in Piedmont Park. In 1998, VHCA members, including Winnie Currie (below), who became a local expert on the building code and its enforcement, helped prevent the redevelopment of the Hilan Theater into the Cotton Club, a large bar. (Left, courtesy of Jack White; below, courtesy of Winnie Currie.)

The Virginia-Highland Neighborhood Commercial District zoning ordinance, passed in 2008, sought a balance between the needs of commercial owners and the community's concerns about density, height, and parking. The effort was spearheaded by VHCA Planning Committee chair John Peak (standing at center) and several steering committee members. It was overwhelmingly approved in an NPU vote. (Courtesy of author.)

Virginia-Highland has been characterized for a half-century by activists known for their service to the community. Today's neighborhood has an active volunteer component, a strong environmental ethic, and many citizens who work closely with municipal and civic boards. Their commitment embodies the spirit that continues to shape the community. (Courtesy of author.)

Visit us at
arcadiapublishing.com

CPSIA information can be obtained
at www.ICGtesting.com
Printed in the USA
LVHW060310030820
662224LV00019B/629